OH, OH! ...and other recent cartoons by

1931-2004

CIAD

GEORGE

ARSIN 04
MONTREAL
THE GAZETTE

Dedicated to the memory of
George Balcan

Enormous love and thanks to my wife Mary Hughson, the very patient designer of this book. Thanks also to Mary's sister Janet Hughson for her editorial help, and to Gaëtan Coté and Pat Duggan at The Gazette *for quality control on a daily basis. Many thanks to Donna Braggins and Gary Hall at* Maclean's *magazine, and to Dick Pound for a wonderful introduction. Former Montrealers Michael Goldbloom, Jack Rabinovitch, Anthony-Wilson Smith and Jennifer Mondoux should be mentioned here for their friendship and assistance. Thanks as always to Kim McArthur, Janet Harron, Debra Schram and the terrific team at McArthur & Company for their relentless enthusiasm and support.*

OH, OH!

...and other recent cartoons by Aislin

With an introduction by Dick Pound

Text by Terry Mosher

McArthur & Company

Toronto

Other books by Aislin:

Aislin–100 Caricatures (1971)
Hockey Night in Moscow (1972, with Jack Ludwig)
Aislin–150 Caricatures (1973)
The Great Hockey Thaw (1974, with Jack Ludwig)
'Ello, Morgentaler? Aislin–150 Caricatures (1975)
O.K. Everybody Take a Valium! Aislin–150 Caricatures (1977)
L'Humour d'Aislin (1977)
The Retarded Giant (1977, with Bill Mann)
The Hecklers: A History of Canadian Political Cartooning
    (1979, with Peter Desbarats)
The Year The Expos Almost Won the Pennant
    (1979, with Brodie Snyder)
Did the Earth Move? Aislin–180 Caricatures (1980)
The Year The Expos Finally Won Something
    (1981, with Brodie Snyder)
The First Great Canadian Trivia Quiz
    (1981, with Brodie Snyder)
Stretchmarks (1982)
The Anglo Guide to Survival in Quebec
    (1983, with various Montreal writers)
Tootle: A Children's Story (1984, with Johan Sarrazin)
Where's the Trough? (1985)
Old Whores (1987)

What's the Big Deal? Questions and Answers on Free Trade
    (1988, with Rick Salutin)
The Lawn Jockey (1989)
Parcel of Rogues (1990, with Maude Barlow)
Barbed Lyres, Canadian Venomous Verse
    (1990, with Margaret Atwood and other Canadian poets)
Drawing Bones–15 Years of Cartooning Brian Mulroney (1991)
Put Up & Shut Up! The 90s so far in Cartoons
    (1994, with Hubie Bauch)
Oh, Canadians! Hysterically Historical Rhymes
    (1996, with Gordon Snell)
One Oar in the Water: The Nasty 90s continued in cartoons
    (1997)
Oh, No! More Canadians! Hysterically Historical Rhymes (1998,
    with Gordon Snell)
2000 Reasons to Hate the Millennium
    (1999, with Josh Freed and other contributors)
The Big Wind-Up! The final book of Nasty 90s cartoons (1999)
Yes! Even More Canadians! Hysterically Historical Rhymes
    (2000, with Gordon Snell)
The Oh, Canadians Omnibus (2001, with Gordon Snell)
More Marvellous Canadians! (2002, with Gordon Snell)
The Illustrated Canadian Songbook, (2003, with Bowser & Blue)

Published in Canada in 2004 by
McArthur & Company 322 King St. West, Suite 402, Toronto, Ontario M5V 1J2 www.mcarthur-co.com

Library and Archives Canada Cataloguing in Publication

Aislin
        Oh, oh!-- and other recent cartoons / Aislin ; introduction by Dick Pound.

ISBN 1-55278-444-4

1. Canada--Politics and government--1993- --Caricatures and cartoons.
2. Canadian wit and humor, Pictorial. I. Title.

NC1449.A37A4 2004   971.064'8'0207   C2004-904243-2

Cover Illustration by AISLIN
Layout, Design, and Electronic Imaging by Mary Hughson
Printed and Bound in Canada by Transcontinental Printing, Inc.

The publisher would like to acknowledge the financial support of the Government of Canada through the Book Publishing Industry Development Program, the Canada Council for the Arts, and the Ontario Arts Council for our publishing activities. We also acknowledge the Government of Ontario through the Ontario Media Development Corporation Ontario Book Initiative.

10 9 8 7 6 5 4 3 2

CONTENTS

Introduction by Dick Pound

We repaired, like truants, to Dunn's, which should be off-limits to those of our generation, but how better to close down those pesky arteries than to ingest a huge, delicious, greasy smoked-meat sandwich – with French fries, of course – a dill pickle and cole slaw for balance?

The official purpose of the exercise, which would be our agreed-upon story for the benefit of our respective spouses, was to discuss with Terry Mosher his forthcoming book of Aislin cartoons. It has been almost three years since his last collection and there is, as might be expected, much from which to choose.

Modern technology allows all his cartoons to be scanned, so before our culinary treat, I was afforded a high-speed overview of the wealth of material from which he would make his final selections. It remains, at the time of writing these words, a moveable feast, since there is much going on that may attract his professional attention.

I asked him how he would define the role of the cartoonist. Think of the cartoonist, he said, as the kid at the back of the class, shooting spit-balls at organizations, people and events. You have to be able to see through pomp and orthodoxy and be willing to point out the ridiculous. Mark Twain expressed the same thought when he said, "Sacred cows make the best hamburger." You may get a detention or two, he said, but the risk is always worth it. I thought, perhaps, that there might be a publishable scientific treatise in this, that I might entitle "The Integrated Theory of Splat," an oft-observed, but never satisfactorily defined branch of the social sciences. But why would I throw away such a scholarly gem in the introduction to someone else's work?

A federal election has been called, the Quebec mega-city referenda are about to be held, there may have been sunstroke victims before the Stanley Cup was awarded in a city in Florida, the nadir of U.S. election politics has not (evidently) yet been reached and baseball players continue to have forearms the size of normal thighs, accompanied by a mantra of denial. The possibilities for exposure to the unerring instinct of the cartoonist are endless. One might think, from their behaviour, that politicians were trained from birth, or possibly were pre-ordained to be fodder for cartoonists. If there is a more satisfying sound than the rapid deflation of a self-inflated politician, it has yet to be catalogued.

'In the can' already are the final years of the Chretien era, the rise and possible fall of Paul Martin, the fall, but refusal to leave, of Bernard Landry, the emergence of Jean Charest, the near-rise and non-rise of the ADQ and a Canadian 'take' on the international and national events of recent years.

The real beauty, however, is the medium. It is easy to ridicule a position, but it takes time and a careful choice of words. The cartoonist proves, every day, that a picture is worth at least a thousand words, especially one that seizes on and magnifies a particular feature of the target – excuse me, the object – of the cartoon, to make the object as ridiculous as the position.

But, shooting fish in a barrel can become too easy and the cartoonist must look everywhere for possibilities – in daily life, in sport and, occasionally, in tragedy. Laughter, like tears, is a means of relieving tensions and others have observed that some things in life are so serious that we can only laugh at them. The cartoonist has the means to allow us to do that, but must be careful only about the timing.

In other subjects, the key is to be timely, where the spit-ball hits the day following the event. The pressure to seize the moment, to visualize the opportunity and then to create it, is remarkable and not for the faint of heart. The cartoonist must have confidence in his instinct to find the jugular and in his craft to illustrate it.

SPEAKING of DRUGS...

Scanning through the output of the last three years of Mosher's work is a trip down recent memory lane. Context comes flooding back, and with it, admiration for the genius that exposed the humorous and the ridiculous at the centre of it.

This is a selection of the work – some of it unpublished prior to this collection – of a Montreal treasure, a Canadian genius who has added immeasurably to the fabric of our society, from the back row of the world's classroom. It is a collection of history and, if newspapers are correctly characterized as the first rough drafts of history, then the cartoonist provides the first rough draft of our murals and frescoes. Laughter, indeed, is the best medicine.

Damn! Have I just been hit with a spit-ball?

Montreal, May 31, 2004

Aislin's cartoon in The Gazette: *September 12, 2001.*

"You know, the world was so simple when we got on the train this morning."

A survivor of the World Trade Center attack,
September 11, 2001

For some reason, I hadn't even tuned my car radio into CBC that morning to catch up on the news during the short drive to work. Instead of plugging into the world, I decided to play a favourite Ben Webster CD. The sun was shining. The music was great. It was a nice day.

As I pulled into The Gazette parking lot, Johnny, the attendant, ran up to the car, talking excitedly about a plane crashing into the World Trade Center. Picturing some navigationally-challenged businessman who banked his Cessna right when he should have banked left, I thought there might be a cartoon in it if no other significant news broke that day.

I reached my studio just in time to switch on CNN and witness the second tower falling. Then, like most of the rest of the world, I sat and watched, transfixed by the horror and the sheer scope of the disaster.

Chapleau's cartoon in La Presse: *September 12, 2001.*

I had to find a way to represent in cartoon form what we had all just experienced. But how do you draw a cartoon with one of the most singularly unfunny events in living memory as the subject? In the end, it seemed right to portray The Statue of Liberty as a silent witness to the catastrophe of the tumbling towers. I wasn't alone. Over the next few days, more than fifty cartoonists from around the world reacted precisely the same way. It was a case of spontaneous 'Yahtzee!'. That's what cartoonists call it when they unknowingly draw the same thing. The exclamation comes from the eponymous game of chance and is used

AllTheNewsThat'sFitableOnThisWebPage.com

Search: Simpler times   Weather: Clear skies   Airport advisory: No delays

Last updated on September 10, 2001

Top News Stories

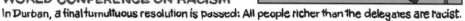

EASTERN SEABOARD
Shark alerts are still in effect along the Atlantic coast.

WORLD CONFERENCE ON RACISM
In Durban, a final tumultuous resolution is passed: All people richer than the delegates are racist.

MAYORALTY RACE
Six people you've never heard of staged a final burst of politicking for tomorrow's New York City primary to replace mayor Rudy Giuliani.

BUSINESS
The latest surge in unemployment has us wondering: Is a crash immenent?

NEW YORK HOPEFULS

SPORTS
Hey, it must be September! Red Sox fold, lose 4th in a row to Yankees. All's well that...

CONDIT — EYES CAUGHT IN KLIEG LIGHTS?

MEDIA
Has CNN gone overboard on its coverage of Gary Condit?

CAREER OPPORTUNITIES
Discover the world from behind a desk! The CIA is looking for undercover operatives. Twenty-three hour work week plus maximum benefits. Must speak fluent American. Apply Langley.

ELSEWHERE
Canada: Progressive Conservative Democratic Representative Coalition is formed. Oh, yawn.

POLL
White House officials have moved to refocus the President's image as a more commanding leader. Question: Is Bush too indecisive?

AGREE   (a) (b) (c) (d) (e)   STRONGLY AGREE

HAPPY BIRTHDAY!
Born on September the 10th: Jose Feliciano and Amy Irving, the voice of Jessica Rabbit.

New on the Web! Information about every building in the New York City database is now available online free of charge: www.NYC.gov/buildings

WE PREFER A DAY THAT DIDN'T CHANGE THE WORLD

AISLIN 01
MACLEAN'S

An imagined web page for September 10, 2001.

when people throw the same number on the dice.

In fact, Serge Chapleau, who works just down the street from me at *La Presse*, Montreal's largest French-language daily, drew the identical image for his newspaper. The next morning, after the cartoons had appeared in our respective papers, Serge called. "So," he asked, "what are we drawing for tomorrow?"

It was a brief light moment, but then we moved on. The next day, I got a little more creative and drew a cartoon that was the first anywhere to depict the two towers as the number eleven.

The outpouring of sympathy for America and Americans was swift and genuine. In the wake of the tragedy, it seemed right that, even if the Americans took the point position, there should be an international police action to hunt down the terrorists. And should the end result be the toppling of Afghanistan's Taliban regime – which had openly supported the terrorist training camps – so be it. We finally became aware of the hardships this regime had visited on its own people and its repression of all Afghanis, but most especially the women of the country. Our new perception of the situation crystalized in the images we saw of Afghani women forced to conceal themselves under burqas.

Canada immediately volunteered to

U.S. offers $25 million reward for the capture Bin Laden.

U.S. drops food-aid packages from the air in Afghanistan.

Bush speech neglects mentioning Canada as a partner.

participate in the Afghanistan action, "shoulder to shoulder" with the Americans and other international forces. But there were tensions between Canada and the U.S. Some in the United States were openly voicing their strong suspicion that anti-American terrorist activities were being organized in Canada, under the very noses of Canadian authorities, and that the September 11th terrorists had in fact been allowed to operate with impunity here. Then President Bush appeared on national television and thanked a long list of countries who had stepped forward to stand at America's side, but omitted to mention Canada. For most Canadians, it was all a bit much after we had extended our hand to all those re-routed passengers and offered our help for the action in Afghanistan. And then, some months later, four Canadian soldiers were killed by an American bomb, so-called "friendly fire". In spite of it all, Canadian forces played and continue to play an important role in Afghanistan.

As I write, the terrorist threat in Afghanistan has not been eliminated and some of the freedoms gained immediately following the ouster of the Taliban regime seem already to have been eroded. America seems to have lost much of its earlier interest in Afghanistan. Its gaze has turned westward, from Kabul to Baghdad.

I really dislike seeing political objectives

Canada agrees to help the U.S. in its war on terrorism in Afghanistan.

Autumn in Afghanistan.

Seventeen out of nineteen soldiers, about to be deployed to Afghanistan, test positive for drug use – and will now be staying home.

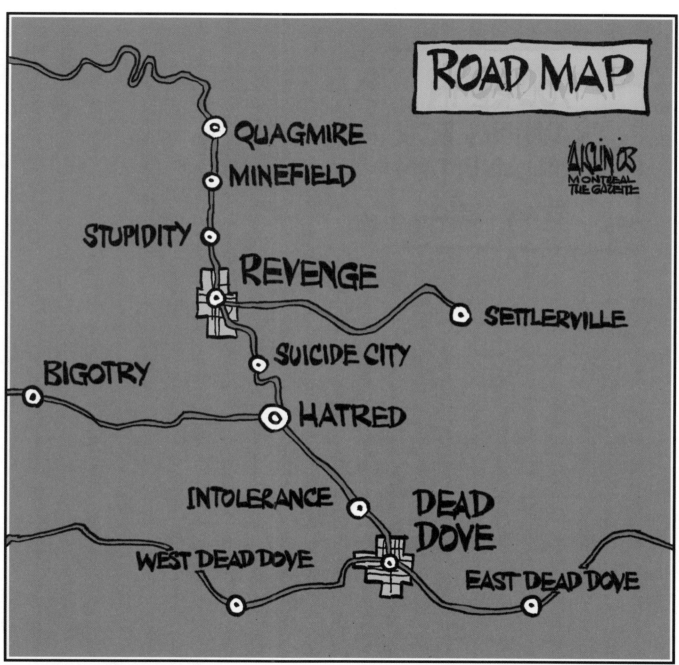

The U.S. proposes a detailed road map to peace in the Middle East.

18

Palestinian suicide bus bombings continue in Israel.

pursued under the cloak of religion. The conflict in the Middle East is obviously complex, but the battle for power and territory always seems to come back to the need to establish the legitimacy of Jewish or Muslim aspirations over those of the other group. My musings on the subject led to my favourite cartoon of the last few years, on the topic of a news item that we never see: Agnostics slaughter Atheists!

Journalist Gwynne Dyer (yeah, the guy in the leather jacket) has written that the 9/11 attacks were intended to raise the profile of radical Islamists in the Muslim world. In his view, another quite specific goal was to lure the United States into invading one or more Muslim countries. Dyer believes that al Qaeda strategists wanted to capture horrifying images of devastating American firepower destroying innocent Muslim lives.
He thinks that Osama bin Laden and his cronies wanted to rekindle the worldwide attention they had garnered while fighting the Russian occupation of Afghanistan. If Dyer is right, has "Bring 'em on!" Bush accomplished Osama's mission?

Like most Canadians, I was relieved when Prime Minster Jean Chrétien announced that Canada would not be participating in the invasion of Iraq. Despite the close relationship between Canada and the U.S. on both personal and political levels, Canadians' feelings towards the United States of America are often ambivalent.

ON the WHITE HOUSE LAWN....

Israel acts up again. Unpublished

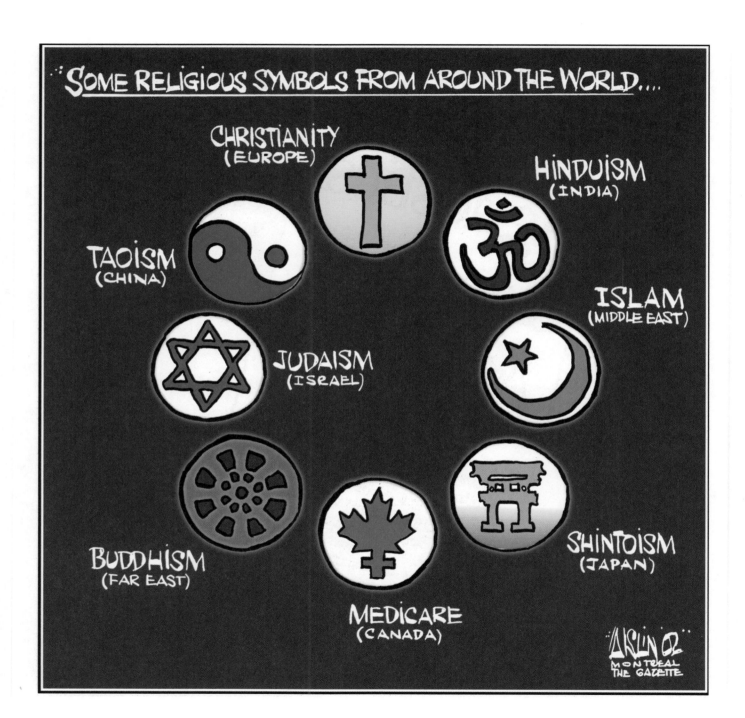

President George W. Bush delivers his State of the Union address.

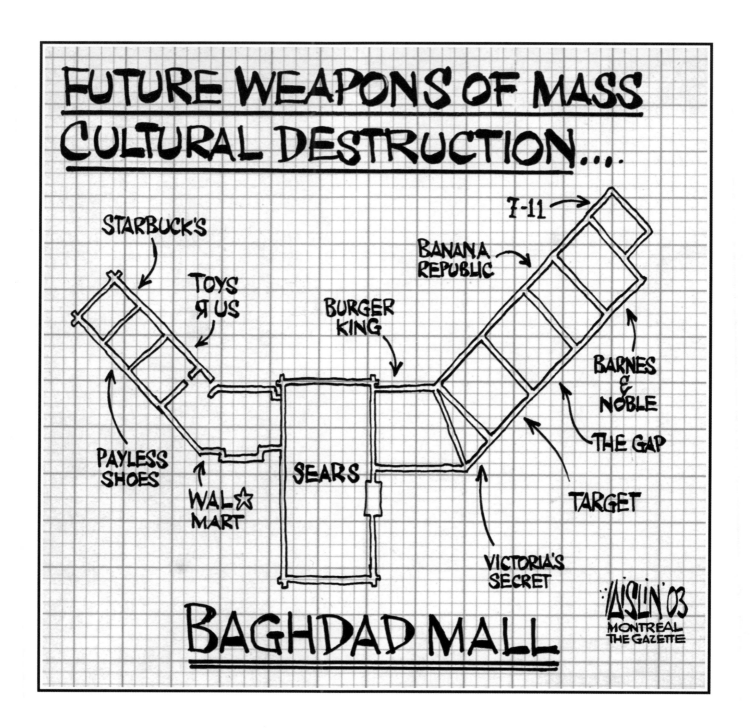

A LITTLE MORE GOOD SENSE TO ALL IN 2003....

WE DID, IN FACT, HAPPEN ON THIS SLINGSHOT, THAT COULD BE CONSTRUED BY GEORGE W. BUSH AS A WEAPON OF MASS DESTRUCTION, ALLOWING HIM TO BLAST IRAQ FROM HERE TO KINGDOM COME—WHICH IS WHY WE LEFT THIS OUT OF OUR FINAL REPORT....

UN INSPECTOR

COLIN POWELL...

UN POSITION on IRAQ....

US POSITION on IRAQ....

BOOM!

Clearly, the concept of NOBLESSE OBLIGE is totally lost on George W. Bush....

HEY! ISN'T THAT FRENCH?

27

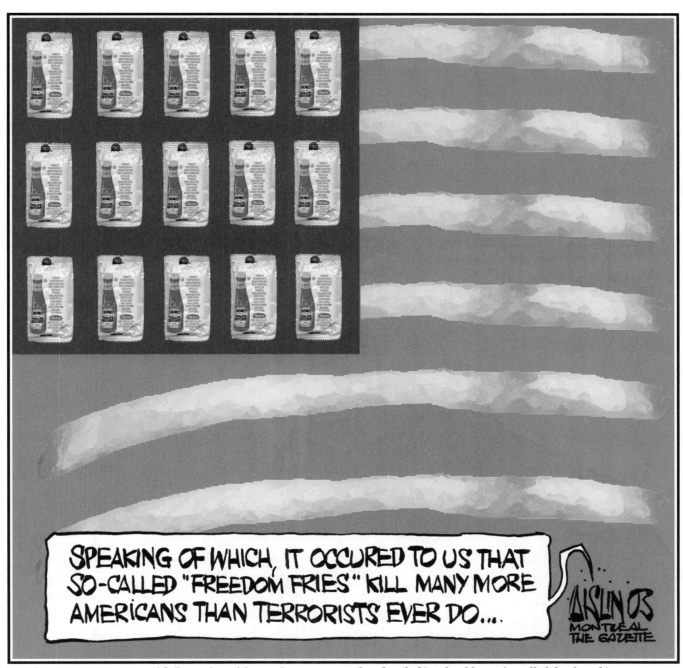

A U.S. congressmen, upset with France's position on Iraq, proposes that french fries should now be called freedom fries.

Colin Powell's presentation to the United Nations suggested strongly that Iraq was hiding weapons of mass destruction.

Anthrax scares plague the U.S. postal service.

Americans told to have duct tape on hand in case of attack.

Terrorism alerts were heightened during the holiday season.

Canadians are told that they should no longer be smiling in their passport photographs.

Saddam Hussein is finally captured by U.S. forces in Iraq.

Iraqi minister insists that the Americans aren't in Baghdad.

Saddam Hussein's hideout is littered with Mars bars wrappers.

Abu Ghraib prison, Iraq.

Actor Arnold Schwarzenegger becomes governor of California.

Ronald Reagan dies, as does…

John Kerry attempts to widen his appeal at the Democratic convention.

The ubiquitous film maker, Michael Moore.

WHITE HOUSE XMAS CARD...

War on Earth!

AISLIN '02
MONTREAL
THE GAZETTE

45

My own sentiments are not anti-American, but rather disappointment that a neighbour which has the power to do so much good in the world is not acting on its potential.

When former U.S. President Bill Clinton accepted a speaking engagement in Montreal in February of 2002, I was quite surprised to be contacted by the organizers of the event. They asked, rather tentatively, if I would draw a cartoon of Clinton and present it to him on stage. "And I suppose you want me to be nice to him?", I asked.

Initially, I declined the invitation. But then my wife pointed out that Clinton's speech would raise a million dollars for a local children's hospital. As Mary put it, "Why not be nice in a cartoon for a change?"

So, I agreed to draw the Clinton cartoon which is shown here on the left.

Everyone – including Clinton – seemed pleased with the gift. But here, on the right, is the cartoon I really wanted to give him.

Canada announces that it will not send troops to Iraq without UN Security Council approval.

CANADA

"This cold, decent country."

Heather Mallick

In what may be remembered as Jean Chrétien's finest moment, the then Prime Minister stood in the House of Commons in March of 2003 to announce that Canada would not be taking part in the American invasion of Iraq. The Bush government went silent on the subject of Canada.

Or did it? Several months later, when a single Black Angus cow in Alberta was found to be infected with bovine spongiform encephalopathy (BSE), the U.S. border was slammed shut to imports of live Canadian cattle. Furthermore, as of the time of writing, the border remains closed at a total cost to the Canadian cattle industry of over $2 billion dollars.

What with BSE, nervousness about the mosquito-borne West Nile virus and the deadly outbreak of SARS in Toronto hospitals, the summer of 2003 was a

difficult one for many Canadians. Add to all that anxiety the menace of terrorism and you have a Canadian tourism industry in free fall – but nowhere so much as in Toronto. In an attempt to fill up the city's empty restaurants, hotels and theatres, Toronto launched an intensive ad campaign, praising its attractions and the great deals to be had. The Rolling Stones were even enticed to give a gala rock concert in suburban Toronto – the lure being either $5 million or $10 million, depending on one's source. The event pulled in some 400,000 visitors.

Canada's independent stand on Iraq was

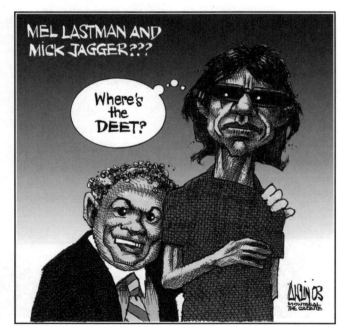

51

SARS benefit rock concert is held in Toronto in front of a well-behaved crowd.

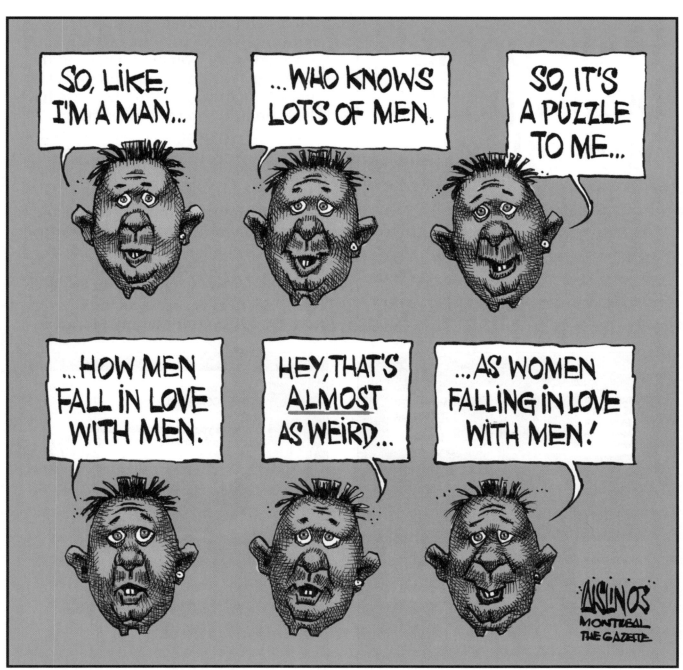

Legalized gay marriages take place in Canada.

Feds' pot is below par: McLellan

MARK KENNEDY
Ottawa Citizen

I MEAN, WITH THE ROLLING STONES COMING IN? WHY CAN'T WE HAVE OUR S**T TOGETHER?

OTTAWA – Ooops! The official supply of federal marijuana is bad weed.

So impure, in fact, that the first crop contains 185 different varieties of pot. Hardly the stuff to provide to seriously ill patients to relieve their symptoms.

Health Minister Anne McLellan revealed the "problem" yesterday, saying it's responsible for the delay – which could last several more months – in getting a much-heralded plan off the ground to provide marijuana to Canad...

Canadian government experiments with pot growing.

OVERHEARD...

THE TRUTH IS, I DON'T EVEN LIKE MARIJUANA VERY MUCH

ME NEITHER. IT MAKES ME FAR TOO DITHERY

BUT I DO LIKE THIS NEW LEGISLATION THAT'S COMING IN HERE IN CANADA. YOU?

OF COURSE! ANYTHING TO PISS OFF THE AMERICANS

An easing of Canada's marijuana laws is proposed.

Letter to the editor
THE ECONOMIST

So glad you now consider Canada to be cool. However, this being January...

noted – and approved – in many countries. Throw into the mix our growing leniency on marijuana and the recent legalization in some provinces of same-sex marriage and suddenly we have The Economist – a magazine often irritatingly dismissive of Canada – calling us "cool." You'll get no argument from me on a January morning in Montreal!

In the summer of 2003, Maclean's magazine thought it might be amusing to commission me – a downtown Montrealer – to do a sketchbook of the Canadian Rockies. My moment of "Mont-réalité" came immediately upon my arrival in Banff. Set next to any peak in the Rockies, it turns out that my Montreal

Canada in January.

mountain is merely a hill. Why I hadn't visited the Rockies before is a bit of a puzzle, having seen most of the rest of Canada – from sea to sea to sea, if you will. Somehow by the end of all previous western swings, I had just wanted to get to Vancouver, my second favourite Canadian city. Consequently, my closest view of the Rockies prior to last July was from 30,000 feet on my way out of Calgary or Edmonton.

Michael Phillips, a retired Canadian diplomat now living in Dublin, had told me that as a teenager, he had waited tables at Jasper Park Lodge. One of his customers was Walt Disney, who claimed that the Banff-Jasper drive was the most beautiful in the world. Whatever else you may say of Walt, he sure knew his vistas.

"If you see a bear, consider <u>not</u> stopping."
JASPER NATIONAL PARK PAMPHLET

OTTAWA

"After all is said and done, a lot more will be said than done."

Unknown

Meanwhile, back in Ottawa the big question of the day was, exactly how long was Jean Chrétien planning to stick around? One suspects that he really didn't want to go at all. After all, any Prime Minister who had won four successive majority governments would normally expect to be asked to stay on as leader for as long as he was on his feet. But this is Canada, and there was a growing feeling in the Liberal Party that it was time for *le p'tit gars de Shawinigan* to move on. Demands that the Prime Minister step aside and call a leadership convention became more insistent following revelations of a number of scandals involving Chrétien-appointed cabinet ministers. There was also an obvious successor waiting in the wings in the person of Paul Martin. Eventually the proponents of change got what they wanted.

FIREARMS PERMIT 2002

Name: Martin Cauchon

Signature:

Type of weapon:

Cost of federal firearms registry rises from $2 million to $1 billion.

Clearly, Canadian Privacy Commissioner George Radwanski liked to dine out.

Revelations that Allan Rock's family was hosted at a luxurious fishing retreat in New Brunswick owned by the Irvings.

Jean Chrétien announces his retirement – sort of.

Finally bending to the pressure generated by the media and his colleagues' leadership aspirations, Jean Chrétien announced in August of 2003 that he would be stepping down as Prime Minister – but not until February 2004! It was the signal for the Prime Minister's Office to get busy establishing the boss's legacy, spending no small amount of money in the process. Finally, the Prime Minister had to acknowledge that his time was up and he would step down in December 2003, immediately following the Liberal Party's leadership convention. He then moved into his new Ottawa condominium within sight of the Parliament buildings. Paul Martin must have been thrilled.

Lame duck.

Jean Chrétien may live in a downtown Ottawa condominium after his retirement.

While the media's focus was firmly on the soap opera of Liberal succession, several of the opposition parties had quietly been manoeuvring themselves into what they hoped would be more effective positions.

Since 1995, the New Democratic Party had been withering on the vine under the sincere, but ineffectual leadership of Alexa McDonough. Her control over certain elements within the party had always seemed tenuous. Svend Robinson in particular always had an agenda uniquely his own. In the summer of 2002, McDonough announced that she would be stepping aside, clearing the way for a leadership race that was won in January 2003 by the media-savvy Toronto city councillor, Jack Layton. It seemed just what the tired old party needed.

During the same period, Canadian conservatives of all stripes alternately coalesced into new factions and then broke away into splinter groups, searching in vain for catchy new names to reflect each reincarnation. As support for the Progressive Conservatives under Joe Clark dwindled, he was replaced as party leader by the feisty Peter MacKay. The Alberta-born Reform Party also reinvented itself, first setting aside its original leader, Preston Manning, and then changing its name to the Canadian Alliance. The popularity of Manning's successor, Stockwell Day, slid fairly rapidly even among his own coterie.

NDP leader passes torch

BY STEVEN CHASE AND JEFF SALLOT, OTTAWA

Federal New Democrats will be asked to choose between returning their party to its left-wing roots or keeping it closer to the political centre in a leadership race touched off yesterday by the resig their chief, Alexa McDo

Ms. McDonough, d in her seven-year term NDP to its former ro ment's third-biggest par

successor's challenge will be to bring "a whole lot more members" into the fold.

"In this particular climate, I think an important attribute of leadership is knowing when to pass the torch," she told reporters.

The NDP, which has 14 seats in he House, averaged 25 seats in ctions from 1962 to 1988, when eaked at 43 seats. In 1993, it won nine seats and has remained urth-largest party in Parliace.

Oh, oh. This time it looks like Svend has finally blown it...

WHAT?

Svend Robinson makes strong Middle-East statements.

JACK...

SLICK...

LOVES...

...the CAMERA!

Joe Clark retires from politics.

Indeed two of the strongest members of Day's caucus led a group of dissident Alliance MPs into a short-lived coalition with the Tories. So Day, too, was forced to make way for a new leader and Stephen Harper took over as Alliance leader in March 2002, becoming Leader of the Opposition that fall. And then...

Brian Mulroney is clearly a background player in the unite-the-right movement.

hell froze over. Despite earlier promises to the contrary and to the accompaniment of much wringing of hands, Stephen Harper and Peter MacKay fused the Canadian Alliance and the Progressive Conservatives into the new Conservative Party of Canada.

The new party's role as the official Opposition was for a time overshadowed by the machinations within the Liberal Party. Indeed, the true opposition to the Chrétien Government seemed to come from within, from the camp of his former Finance Minister, Paul Martin.

In the late 1980s, Paul Martin had stepped out of the business world and into

Two right feet.

Belinda Stronach, of auto parts fame, runs for the leadership of the new Conservative Party.

Stephen Harper wins the Conservative Party leadership race.

politics, starting his long campaign to become Prime Minister. At the time, he seemed a somewhat bland figure. In contrast to many politicians of the day, there was no defining feature that stood out. So I drew several cartoons of him with just an outline and no face. Mark Abley, one of *The Gazette's* best feature writers at that time, was assigned to write a major profile of Mr. Martin, who, at the close of the interview, asked Abley to pass on a message. "You tell that Aislin that I really am interesting!" Indeed.

Canadians have spent years waiting for this coronation. That Paul Martin deserved to be Prime Minister after nine extremely successful years as Minister of Finance has been so thoroughly drummed into us that it seemed no less than his destiny. And no one appeared to believe this more surely than Paul Martin himself.

Still, we live in a democracy, so there had to be at least the appearance of a competition for the Liberal Party's top job. Three members of Cabinet – Allan Rock, John Manley and Sheila Copps – expressed varying degrees of interest in running for the leadership. And where are they now? Copps actually had the audacity to pursue the leadership right to the bitter end, only to be banished from the party. The more discreet Allan Rock was named Canada's Ambassador to the United Nations, while John Manley was appointed by Ontario's

John Manley replaces Paul Martin as Minister of Finance.

Paul Martin's first order of business.

Paul Martin's favourite meal is Kraft Dinner™.

Premier to a Royal Commission on the province's energy system.

In December 2003, Paul Martin officially took over the reigns of power from Jean Chrétien, evidently counting on a quiet transition. However, the waters quickly got choppy. First it was disclosed that over the previous eleven years, Canada Steamship Lines, a company owned by Paul Martin, had received $161 million in government money, a figure one thousand times greater than originally reported.

Even more damaging was a report issued by Canada's Auditor General, Sheila Fraser, in early February 2004. It confirmed that three Quebec ad agencies had pocketed

over $100 million in government contracts and commissions while Jean Chrétien was still Prime Minister. Some of the invoices appeared to have no foundation in actual work. And this 'adscam' report had legs! It angered the Canadian people to such an extent that the Liberals were hung with it all through the winter and into the spring of 2004.

Martin did his best to confront these issues, travelling from one end of the country to another to try and calm the waters. Between many promises to get to the bottom of the 'sponsorship scandal' and commitments on health care, the Prime Minister laid the groundwork for an

It is revealed that Canadian Steamship Lines received a thousand times more government money than was originally reported.

Alfonso Gagliano resists returning from Denmark.

Gagliano appears before the commons sponsorship committee.

The adscam scandal…

…but who knew?

Critics claim that Mel Gibson's controversial film The Passion *suggests that the Jews turned on Christ.*

Paul Martin goes on a media campaign to try and quell the storm.

Paul Martin criss-crosses the country during Easter to try and shore up support.

expected spring election.

Just when all bets were off on the election call, the Prime Minister bit the bullet and declared that June 28, 2004 would be the day. It was odd timing, in that it fell precisely between Quebec's St. Jean Baptiste celebration and Canada Day. It's a time of year when most Canadians don't want to think about politics.

The election was a rough-and-tumble affair with some fairly serious accusations being hurled about. At the outset, the Liberal campaign had little traction and it seemed that the newly-formed Conservative Party might even win a slim majority.

The NDP also seemed likely to make substantial gains under the high-energy leadership of Jumpin' Jack Flash Layton. And the Bloc Québecois was more than happy to benefit from Quebec voters' anger over the sponsorship scandal.

In the end, all the parties got at least a bit of what they wanted. Canadians pulled back from the brink of dramatic change and re-elected the Liberals under Paul Martin, albeit with a minority. The Bloc equalled its highest ever proportion of seats, and both the Conservatives and New Democrats improved their fortunes. It's the Canadian compromise.

With that job done, Canadians promptly turned their attention to the important business of enjoying summer, and nowhere so much as in my Montreal...

Election called for June 29th, 2004.

The Liberals drop badly in the polls during the first few weeks of the election.

Stephen Harper, known for his pro-American views, can smell victory.

Jack Layton held Paul Martin personally responsible for the deaths of homeless people.

A Conservative-Bloc alliance is speculated upon, even if Gilles Duceppe is not a Calgary Flames fan.

The Marijuana Party's catchy slogan.

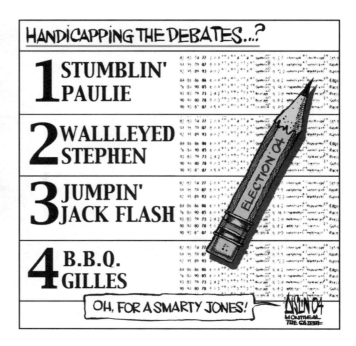

The Conservatives blow it at campaign's end.

A minority government seems likely.

Canada votes.

MONTRÉAL

"This is the city for me. This is paradise."
Jackie Robinson, on Montreal

More than any other metropolis in Canada, Montreal is a street city. We love the outdoor urban life and thumb our noses at winter by jamming as much street activity into the fair weather months as possible. There's something for everyone. In the summer of 2004, Montreal's famous Cirque du Soleil – which started life as a collective of street performers – celebrated its 20th anniversary. Since our Jazz Festival, with its usual array of excellent open air concerts, was marking its twenty-fifth year in operation at the same time, the two combined for a fantastical street celebration of music and magic. There's more: the international fireworks competition, the Formula One race, Just for Laughs shenenigans… It should come as no surprise then that our excellent restaurants and terrasses and the unsurpassed opportunity they provide for

Gerald Tremblay plays the financial blues.

people watching, combined with a seemingly endless parade of summer festivals – all of it offered with a certain European flair – make tourism Montreal's number one industry today.

The city's economy has recently experienced a mini-boom, particularly in the hi-tech industries, and this has resulted in a re-invigorated real estate market.

The creative energy which is apparent in both traditional business and new technology sectors, as well as in the cultural milieu, thrives in spite of antiquated municipal governance. No matter which party is in power, the health of Montreal's infrastructure and community programs is solely dependant on the whims of an already financially-squeezed provincial government in Quebec City. If Quebec City is on the verge of a cold, Montreal sneezes first.

Montreal's current mayor, Gerald Tremblay, is faced with the same permanent cash-crunch dilemma as all his predecessors. On top of that, he has been trying to deal with the city's notoriously confrontational municipal workers' union, known as les cols bleus. With road repairs proceeding at an achingly slow pace, the streets of Montreal seem frozen in permanent grid-lock.

No doubt about it – Montreal's infrastructure is crumbling.

Montreal's ongoing comedy festival.

MONTREAL'S MAYOR...

Hells Angels' leader, Mom Boucher is sentenced to life in jail.

MSO director Charles Dutoit resigns his post.

Punks set fire to cars after rock concert cancellation.

In Montreal, both the Highland Games and Gay Pride Day are held on the same day in August.

Huge potholes, traditionally a rite of spring, have now become a year-round headache. One wag has suggested that Montreal add to its already impressive festival line-up with an on-going homage to the city's potholes.

On the other hand, city residents have been happy to note progress in tackling other serious problems endemic to this town. Montreal is no longer the crime capital it once was. After a concerted joint campaign by a number of police forces, many Hells Angels have been convicted of major crimes and thrown in jail. Of particular note, the gang's leader, Mom Boucher, was convicted of murder in May 2002 and handed an automatic life sentence.

The face of Montreal has changed dramatically over the last fifteen years due to an influx of new residents from all over the world. Once lumped by government and media into a linguistic grab-bag known as allophones, these new Montrealers are now moving into positions of influence and responsibility in various fields.

The St. Patrick's Day parade is very popular in Montreal.

St. Patrick's Day, Montreal.

Anne Myles: The new soft-spoken Anglo advocate.

Thankfully, the bitter language wars of yesteryear seem to have died away into occasional spats that provide much-needed comic diversion. Recently, a blind Quebecker who had registered for English immersion classes at the University of New Brunswick was later refused entry because his guide dog would only respond to commands in French. After the storm of media attention, the University caved in and allowed both dog and master to join the class.

This caricature was drawn by Aislin in 1983 as a cover illustration for a best-selling book on Anglo paranoia.

In 2002, Télé-Québec asked Aislin for an updated cartoon on how he viewed the English today for a film on Anglo culture.

The more harmonious linguistic environment has prodded Montreal's English-speaking population into waking up and smelling the café au lait. Many Anglos had reacted nervously – and badly – following the narrowly-defeated 1995 referendum on Quebec sovereignty. Now most of those shrill voices have either gone silent or moved out of range. The newer generation of Anglos seems far more comfortable with Montreal's French identity and growing multi-racial character. But don't ask them to give up their comfy little towns!

FOR THOSE OF YOU DISENCHANTED WITH THE PQ, THE ADQ AND JEAN CHAREST, WE ARE PROUD TO ANNOUNCE A BRAND NEW POLITICAL PARTY....

'Ta-dah!' LE PARTLY QUÉBÉCOIS

OH, AND INCIDENTALLY, MY QUEBEC INCLUDES VERMONT

AND VPR!

AISLIN 02
MONTREAL
THE GAZETTE

In 2000, the Parti Québecois introduced Bill 170. Intended to force a number of Quebec municipalities to merge into five major metropolitan areas, its biggest impact would be felt in Montreal. The concept of "one island, one city" had been enthusiastically promoted by Montreal's mayor at that time, Pierre Bourque.

However, just before Bill 170 was brought into law on January 1, 2000, Bourque was defeated in a municipal election by Gerald Tremblay, whose position on the subject of a mega-merger was far more ambiguous.

Similarly, the Parti Québecois was defeated in 2003 by Liberal Jean Charest. As part of his election platform, Charest promised to allow forcibly amalgamated municipalities to hold de-merger referenda.

A significant number of suburban citizens were furious over the forced mergers, which they viewed as undemocratic and little more than a massive tax grab on the part of the City of Montreal. (Yeah, but how else were we going to repair those potholes?)

Both Tremblay and Charest were actually in favour of the mega-merger, but to meet their respective election promises, they had to follow through on organization of a de-merger vote. Those communities that wished to put the

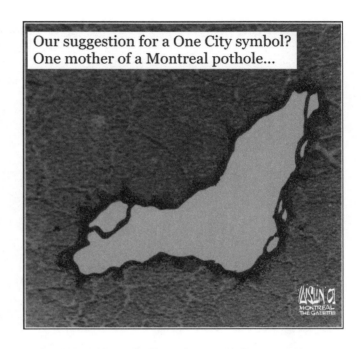

ITEM: CITY WILL KILL TWO BIRDS....

(Umm. Let's rephrase that, shall we?)

ITEM: CITY WILL DEAL WITH TWO ISSUES BY SHELTERING HOMELESS PERSONS IN POTHOLES

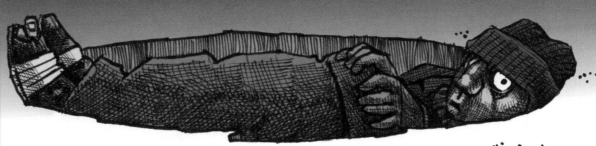

AISLIN 04
MONTREAL
THE GAZETTE

question to their residents held referenda in June 2004. Whereas most chose to remain with their new municipalities, fifteen of Montreal's twenty-two suburbs voted to cede from the mega-Montreal.

"One island, sixteen cities", as *The Gazette* wrote the following day.

The vast majority of these fifteen suburbs are located in the west end of Montreal, home to most of the city's English-speaking population. And even though the argument was made – mostly by Anglophones – that the de-merger vote was not a French-English issue, the results in Westmount, Town of Mount Royal, Point Claire and Beaconsfield would indicate otherwise.

In the end, the votes seem largely symbolic. Under the new arrangement, the fifteen solitudes will still end up forking over the vast majority of their tax revenues to the City of Montreal.

Lucien Bouchard's proposal for a new Montreal waterfront.

116

THE INCREDIBLE SHRINKING MAN...

QUÉBEC

"I know that you believe that you understand what you think I said, BUT I am not sure you realize that what you heard is not what I meant!"

Bernard Landry

Although the voices of those who dream of Quebec sovereignty have grown fainter over the years, the concept continues to permeate all Quebec political thought and action.

Recently, the most barbed attacks from members of the province's *souverainiste* political classes have been aimed not at Canada, but at other factions within their own Parti Québecois.

Benoît Aubin, a popular Quebec journalist, makes this analysis: "Quebeckers want a father figure premier, someone who is above the fray."

Non-stop bickering creates rifts within the Parti Québécois.

119

On September 8, 2002, Bernard Landry declared that Quebec would be a sovereign country in one thousand days.

So it is that Quebeckers have elected premiers like René Lévesque, Robert Bourassa and Lucien Bouchard. But staying "above the fray" doesn't work for ever when there is serious in-fighting. Lucien Bouchard decided to back away from the premiership when the going got too rough, whereupon the Parti Québecois (PQ) handed the reins to a party stalwart, the inconsistent Bernard Landry.

Anxious to legitimize his leadership, and with the PQ up in the polls for a brief time, Landry called an election for April 2003.

Immediately prior to the election call, Landry dramatically announced that the clock was now ticking down on "one thousand days to sovereignty!" Typically, the party retreated somewhat during the election campaign, adjusting the slogan to: "One thousand days to *union confédérale!*", whatever that is.

Jean Charest, the former leader of Canada's Progressive Conservative Party, had come home to Quebec in April 1998 to take over as leader of the Provincial Liberal Party. Having tirelessly stumped throughout the province in the interim, Charest led his team into the spring 2003 election campaign under the confident slogan: "We are ready."

Right turns on red now allowed in some regions of Quebec.

Production of the once-popular Camaro is halted.

The Quebec election is called for April 15, 2003.

Bernard Landry is known to blow the occassional gasket.

Mario Dumont, leader of the fledgling Action Démocratique Party, entered the campaign with a surprising lead in the polls which he lost as soon as the campaign heated up.

Less than enamoured with the PQ's continual internal bickering – and as Jacques Parizeau imposed himself yet again on the party's campaign strategy – Quebec voters expressed their frustration and boredom with the party, somewhat grudgingly turning to Jean Charest and his neo-conservative team.

Charest's first year in power has been a bumpy ride. He has fumbled with the controls of the very complicated Quebec political and bureaucratic machine. In the face of labour protests and voter dissatisfaction, his popularity, which was never robust, plunged dramatically. Nevertheless, he has time to turn things around. The next Quebec election is still at least several years away. Much will depend on who is chosen to lead the Parti Québécois into the next campaign.

Jaques Parizeau expresses himself during the election.

Once leading in the polls, the ADQ wins only four seats.

Bernard Landry's Parti Québécois loses the election.

After losing the election, the P.Q. must move offices.

After several frusrating attempts, the Montreal Alouettes finally win the 2002 Grey Cup.

SPORTS

"It is not the size of the dog in the fight that counts, but the size of the fight in the dog."

Archie Griffin

Montreal loves its pro sports, even if the teams themselves sometimes fall out of favour. That is why the success of the reincarnated Alouettes – who brought the Grey Cup home in 2002 – has been a real shot in the arm for despairing sports fans. For Montreal, a city once famous for its wealth of championship teams, has been living through a drought.

A case in point is the sorry tale of our major league baseball franchise. The Montreal Expos, a fixture here since 1969, had for a while posted solid results and earned fans' enthusiastic support. Players were embraced as hometown heroes, although admittedly most were American or Latin-American.

Larry Smith thinks of running for the Conservative leadership.

OLD SAN JUAN....

PARE

ARRIBA!

LOOKING OUT FOR NATIONAL TREASURE, JOSE VIDRO

POLICIA

VIDRO 3

A MASCARA DEL VEGIGANTE MAY BE WORN LOCALLY TO WARD OFF EVIL SPIRITS, BUT IT DIDN'T WORK ON THE BRAVES...

WARNING: PARE means STOP in Spanish. In Puerto Rico it means MAYBE-WE'LL-SLOW-DOWN or MAYBE-WE-WON'T.

Serie De LOS EXPOS

More like LOST Expos

SOUVENIR CAP

THE MOST IMPORTANT PERSON OFF THE FIELD? EXPO SCORER MICHEL "SPINNER" SPINELLI

A San Juan, Puerto Rico, sketchbook drawn during a Montreal Expos home stand being played there.

Expos go on a brief winning streak in August of 2003.

But then Charles Bronfman sold the team to a consortium of new owners in 1991, setting the scene for some truly unfortunate management decisions, including the eventual resale to New Yorker Jeffrey Loria. Initially hailed as a saviour, Loria ended by being despised for stripping the team of talent before going off to buy the Florida Marlins, thereby forcing major league baseball to baby-sit the Expos franchise. Not surprisingly, support for the "Spos" sank to an all-time low. With the team turning into a novelty act, the last few years in Montreal have been painful. In the League's desperation to get more fans out to games, we have even had to suffer the indignity of sharing home-team status with San Juan, Puerto Rico, which hosted twenty-two of the Expos' home games in each of the last two seasons. It will almost be a relief when the League finally announces that the team will be moved to Washington or Virginia. (The final decision had still not been made as of this book's deadline for publication).

Major league baseball has faced a number of other thorny problems. The rules governing the behaviour of baseball players have never been as stringent as those applied to other pros when it comes to drug use, especially steroids. But how can we continue to turn a blind eye to players' unaccountably pumped-up

...that is the question.

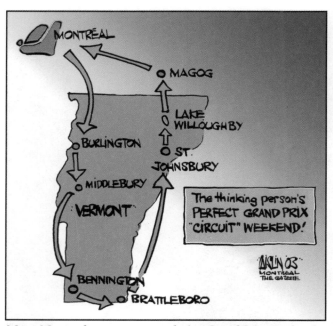

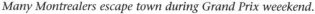
Many Montrealers escape town during Grand Prix weeekend.

physiques and the unprecedented pace at which new home run records are being set? Clearly, the leagues will have to deal with the issue of power-enhancing drugs sooner rather than later.

Montreal's increasingly diverse population is having an impact on the city's sports interests. It looks, for example, as though soccer could one day beat out football as summer's spectator sport of choice. The city's European sensibility is reflected in the popularity of the annual Grand Prix. The race is held over one weekend every June and has the biggest draw of any single sporting event in town, attracting over 300,000 visitors each year.

However, none of this was helping to offset Montrealers' decade-long despondency about the performance of their legendary hockey team. So far had we fallen that we were practically delirious when the Habs actually made the playoffs in 2002, admittedly in eighth place. Unable to produce a winning franchise, the team had to fall back on reminding fans of the glory days just to sell some tickets.

Canadian men's and women's teams both win gold medals at the Salt Lake City Olympics.

Veteran Gazette sports writer, Red Fisher, picks his all-time Montreal Canadiens all-star team.

But then – hallelujah! – former Habs great Bob Gainey was named General Manager in June 2003. His impressive track record with other teams was cause for some optimism about the Canadiens' future. Following Gainey's first season at the helm (2003-2004), that confidence seems well-placed. The entire organization has begun to function more as a team; players have even demonstrated occasional flashes of brilliance. Montreal dares to dream of a brighter hockey future.

Habs make the playoffs in 2002.

The game of hockey itself has had its ups and downs over the last three years. In 2002, the entire nation celebrated great Olympic victories by both the men's and women's teams in Salt Lake City.

In 2004, the imagination of the country was fired once again as the Calgary Flames, underdogs at season's opening, came within a hair of bringing the Stanley Cup home to Canada. Could we have given such wholehearted support to the Maple Leafs? In another good news story, Alberta's capital hosted a different sort of hockey game when the Habs and Oilers played before a record crowd – outdoors!

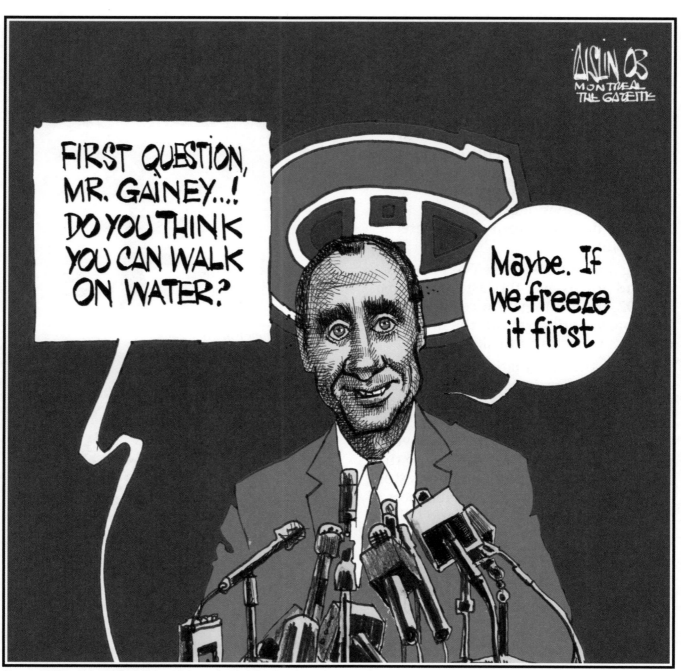

Former Habs great, Bob Gainey, is named general mamager of Les Canadiens.

The Habs' performance improves dramatically.

57,000 fans watch NHL hockey being played outdoors.

…hating The Toronto Maple Leafs.

Canada goes wild over the Calgary Flames reaching the finals.

141

Still, nothing has been done about the sport's biggest problem. No, I don't mean Don Cherry.

I mean the violence. The rough play that has always been part of hockey in this country is a far cry from the sheer brutality we witnessed on March 8, 2004 when Vancouver Canuck Todd Bertuzzi attacked Steve Moore of the Colorado Avalanche. The nasty check from behind broke Moore's neck and caused other significant injuries.

Even though Bertuzzi was suspended by the NHL for the remainder of the season and may face jail time, he has the easier fate – Moore may never play again.

A cynic would say that the NHL will likely take minimal action as a result of this incident since violence seems to put bums in seats.

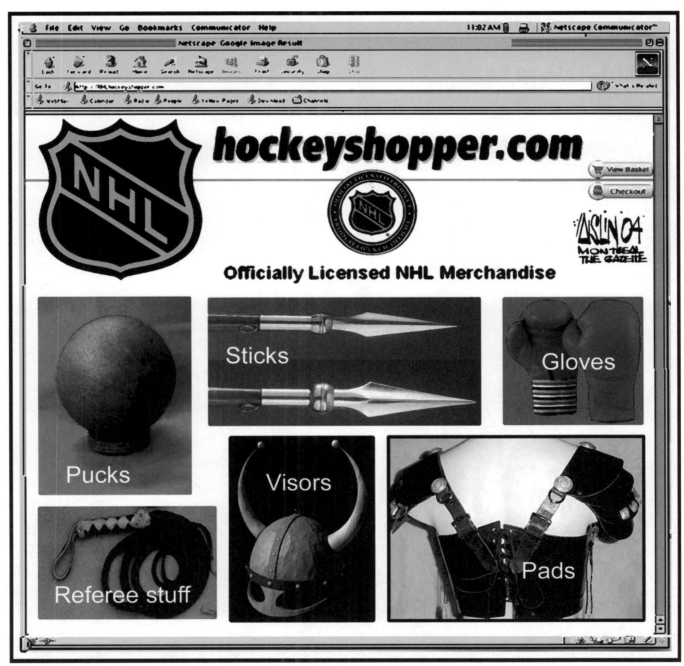

A proposed new web site for the National Hockey League.

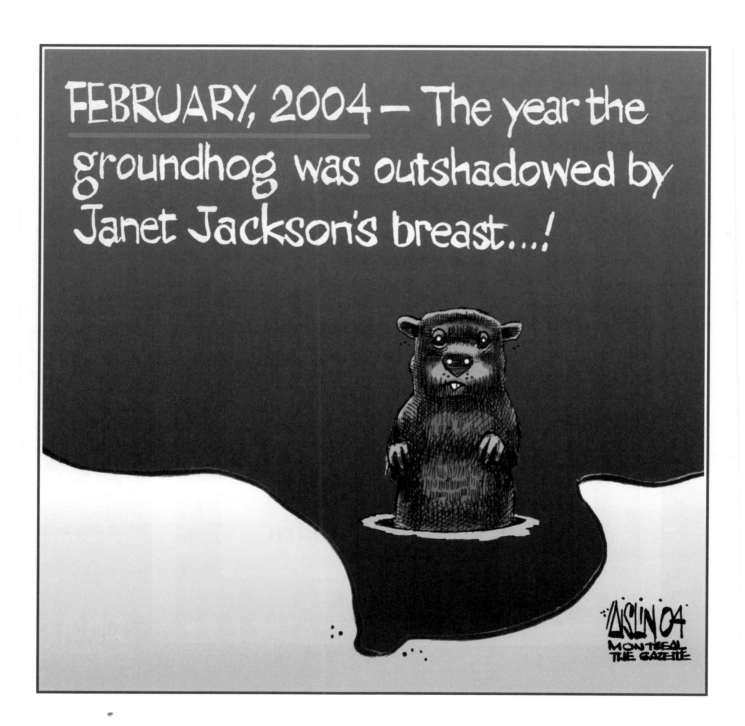

*"Love the company all you want.
Just understand that the company
doesn't love you."*

Anonymous

What could possibly make America's annual advertising extravaganza – the Super Bowl – any more of a spectacle than it already is? Thanks to the February 2004 edition, we now know. Forget about which corporation paid more bucks for a 30-second promo spot or which team played the better football. The clear winner was of course Janet Jackson. That calculated little flash of the right breast during the half-time show did more to hype her new album than any bottomless advertising budget could ever have accomplished.

In contrast, brother Michael's sales have been tanking. His once merely eccentric lifestyle has degenerated into perverse self-indulgence and the chickens have finally come home to roost. The public is generally forgiving of its pop idols, but it's hard to defend a man who openly admits to sleeping with young boys. The story prompted me to draw this (unpublished) cartoon of Michael Jackson as a Catholic priest on the next page.

The analogy is sadly appropriate. Over the last few years, the Catholic Church has been forced to acknowledge damning allegations of sexual abuse by priests, the cases almost too numerous to count. The scope of this scandal can only be enormously embarrassing and hurtful for

Unpublished

ITEM: POPE SUMMONS AMERICANS...

American cardinals discuss scandals with the Pope in Rome.

SOMETHING WE'D LIKE TO SEE AT WORLD YOUTH DAY

Women in the priesthood?

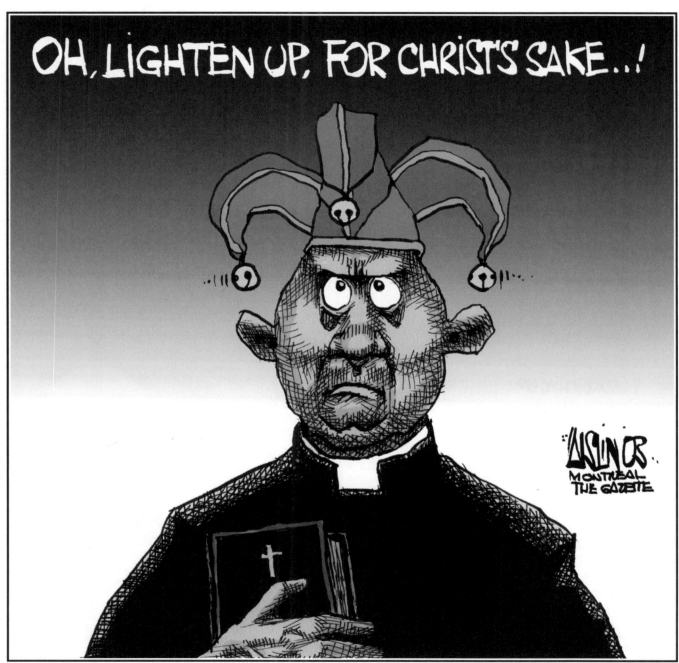

The Catholic Church denounces homosexuality.

the Pope and devout Catholics everywhere. It's all a little ironic given the Church's indignant denunciation of homosexuality. Lots of us also have difficulty getting our minds around the Catholic Church's continuing refusal to ordain female priests and indeed to give women a full and equal role in its hierarchy. The Bible exerts a powerful force for good and ill. Is it time for Christians to adopt a new play book?

Some people dig in their heels to avoid change and some embrace it. But for a rapidly aging population – the declining birth rate in Canada has pushed our average age to over 40 – it is not always easy to keep up. We do our best to accommodate the constant "improvements" in our world but every day we're faced with some new technology we supposedly can't live without.

It's in the communications sector that things have really gotten out of hand. Not a minute is wasted. Answer your e-mail as you walk the dog, call your broker while you're stuck at the traffic light, download your entire life onto your Blackberry and feel good about being Googled. What would you make of today's world if you were just emerging from 5 years of hibernation?

Release of The Lord of The Rings *movies attracts keen fans from all age groups.*

TONIGHT ON "NOT UNINTERESTING CANADIAN BOOKS," WE HAVE AN EXCITING LINEUP...,

① MARGARET ATWOOD WITH HER NEW NOVEL "ORYX AND CRAKE"..

② WALTER STEWART ON HIS NEW BIOGRAPHY OF TOMMY DOUGLAS...

③ CELEBRITY CHEF, FRANK COTRONI DEMONSTRATES AMAZING THINGS HE CAN DO WITH A MEAT CLEAVER!

Frank Cotroni has written a cookbook.

Thank heavens we still have books! In fact, we're printing more of them every year. The problem is that we're reading a lot fewer of them. Maybe everyone's waiting for the movie. The publishing industry is headed for a major crisis and I feel for all my good friends in the business.

Here in Canada, we're finally catching on that it's a good thing to celebrate our writers and our books.

Every November, I have the pleasure of attending the Giller Awards in Toronto. It's a gala event, with lots of schmoozing and a great meal. But for the trainload of Montrealers who make the journey each year, it's all about Doris.

Doris Giller was a force to be reckoned with when I got to know her in the early 1980s. In those days, she was the Montreal *Gazette's* revolutionary book editor, a loud and lively member of a raucous crew that hung out at the Montreal Press Club. That gang included Mordecai Richler, Nick Auf der Maur, Ian Mayer and any number of other reprobates. But then, Doris began hanging around with some interloper called Jack Rabinovitch. Didn't she up and marry the crafty devil and disappear down the 401 with him – to despised Toronto to boot?

In the end, we forgave Jack for stealing Doris away. For after she died far too early in 1993, Jack and Mordecai Richler

At the Giller Awards.

dreamed up the Giller tribute and it has become Canada's must-do literary happening. Doris would have loved the whole thing: a grandiose event devised by Mordecai and paid for by Jack, all the fuss, the preening and fawning and – most of all – the indefinable Toronto-ness of it all.

The newspaper world was shocked when in September 2000, a cash-strapped Conrad Black sold a major portion of the Southam newspaper chain to the Asper family of Winnipeg. It must have hurt – whatever Black's faults, he really loved those newspapers. The Aspers, on the

The Aspers introduce "national editorials." Unpublished

The Aspers feud with the CBC.

other hand, have always been more interested in television as a medium and own the Global network. They ruffled some feathers with their determination to import television's focus on the bottom line to the newspaper business.

Then they made a really controversial decision. Traditionally, owners have trusted individual papers to determine their own editorial policy, but the Aspers insisted that all the newly acquired papers print "National Editorials" conceived at head office. Much consternation ensued. No doubt the family was not used to their staff biting back. The national editorials did appear for a while, but have blessedly gone the way of the dodo.

While all this was going on, Conrad Black and certain members of his board of directors were accused of appropriating rather too large a portion of company profits. For many, Black's fall from grace came to epitomize rampant corporate and individual avarice in North America's private sector.

CEOs are being fired right, left and centre and in some cases, serving time. Do their transgressions represent a new trend or have we just been blind?

The rest of us might as well live in a different universe. Nonetheless, we're being told over and over that we've never been better off. Well okay, maybe if we try

Conrad Black has financial difficulties.

Quebec convenience store chain Couche-Tarde buys up 1,663 new stores in the U.S.

In Jonquière, Quebec, the first Wal-Mart store is unionized.

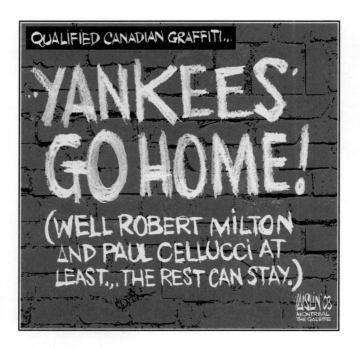

just sitting here and not moving. What are the alternatives? Have you flown Air Canada recently? Filled your car at the gas pump?

Perhaps that's the answer. We might simply park more. Be still, or – at the very least – stiller.

Until the next book...

Terry Mosher (Aislin)
Montreal
August 7, 2004

House prices continue to escalate.

Will Molson merge with Coors?

167

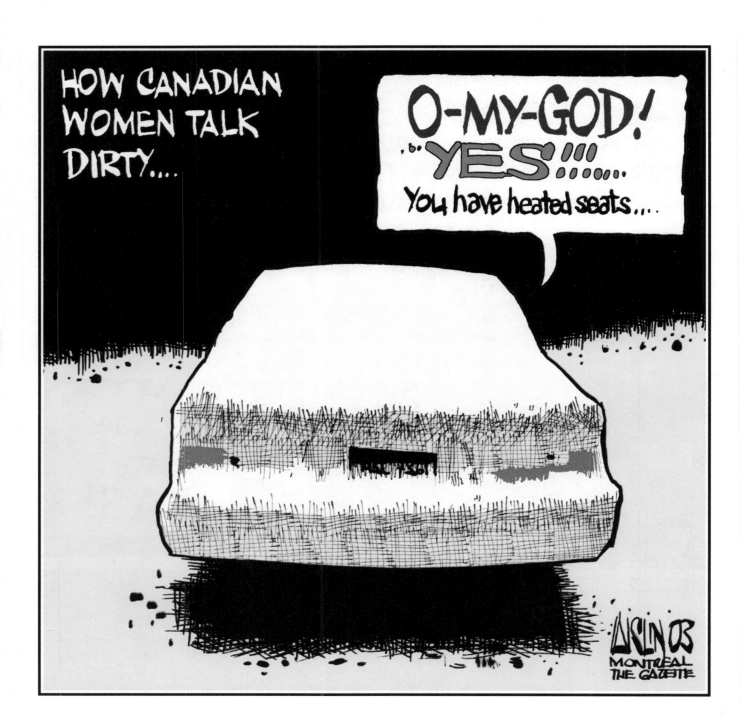